The Song of Songs

Also by Marcia Falk

Am I Also You?
    Translations from the Yiddish Poetry
    of Malka Heifetz Tussman

The
Song of Songs

Love Poems from the Bible

Translated from the Original

Hebrew by Marcia Falk

Harcourt Brace Jovanovich

New York and London

Illustrations by Barry Moser

Printed in the United States of America

Grateful acknowledgment is made to *Response*, *Barrow*, and
Moment in which some of these poems first appeared.

Library of Congress Cataloging in Publication Data
Bible. O. T. Song of Solomon. English. Falk. 1977.
   The Song of songs.
   Based on the translator's thesis, Stanford.
   I. Falk, Marcia. II. Title.
BS1487.F34 1977   223'.9'052   77–73049
ISBN 0–15–183770–8

First edition

B C D E

Isaac Bashevis Singer once said, "If there is one thing the Jewish people has never suffered from, it's amnesia." I agree, but I would add that neither have we suffered from a lack of vision. To our future, then, as well as to our past—to our poets, our prophets, and all those who transmit the tradition of the books in the daily journeys of their lives—I dedicate this translation.

Acknowledgments

"All journeys have secret destinations of which the traveler is unaware."* I began my study of the Song of Songs in 1971, under the guidance of Prof. Edwin Good of the Religious Studies Department at Stanford University. At that time I was doing graduate work in the Stanford English Department and, quite apart from my interest in the Song, I was beginning to work on verse translation. At the suggestion of several members of the Stanford English Department, I decided to merge my study of the Song with my developing commitment to translation; the result was, after five years, a verse translation of the Song with an accompanying critical commentary that together comprised my doctoral thesis. I am grateful to the Stanford English Department for allowing and supporting this rather unusual dissertation, and in particular I thank my thesis advisors, Profs. John Felstiner and Ronald Rebholz, for their patient scrutiny of the several drafts of my work. I was fortunate to have Prof. Good as my third advisor; he not only introduced me to the exciting possibilities of combining Bible study with literary analysis but guided the dissertation from inception to completion.

Several other scholars also helped at various stages along the way. I thank Prof. Chaim Rabin, of the Hebrew Language Department at the Hebrew University in Jerusalem, for answering my queries about obscure words in the original and for sharing with me his fascinating theories on the Song. Dr. Nogah Hareuveni, biologist and director of Neot Kedumim: The Gardens of Israel, advised me on the controversial matters of identifying flora and fauna in the Bible; many of my

* Martin Buber.

interpretations were influenced by the new findings made available to me by Dr. Hareuveni and members of his staff. And I am deeply grateful to Prof. Moshe Greenberg, of the Bible Department at the Hebrew University, for discussing and debating with me my interpretations of the Song before even seeing my translations, and later for encouraging me to persevere at them.

Of course, valuable help also came from poets, both those who read my work and those whose work I read and learned from. In particular I am grateful to my dear friend Margaret Fountain Edwards for so generously offering me the benefit of her critical eye and fine poetic sensibilities, and to Kenneth Fields for his many thoughtful criticisms and suggestions when the work was in its early stages.

I wish to acknowledge the Fulbright-Hays Foundation and the Israeli Government for a combined grant which supported my research in 1973–74, and Stanford University for fellowship assistance.

For various kinds of aid and advice, special thanks to the following people: Steven Axelrod, Betty Brereton, T. Carmi, Everett Fox, Prof. Nahum Glatzer, Gerry Gould, William Novak, Eleanor Schick, and Mary K. Wakeman. Personal thanks to many other friends who were there when the road was rocky. For continued faith that I could always count on—thank you, Sam. And to my parents, who were my first teachers, thank you for pointing the way.

To Barry Moser, the artist who illustrated this book, goes my gratitude for the care he took to engross himself in the translations before setting his own pen to paper. And my appreciation to my editor, Gayle Benderoff, for her vision and her enthusiasm.

To all who have guided the journey, I am grateful.

For all flaws in the work, however, I accept full responsibility. Whatever is strong in this translation attests, above all, to the timeless power of its source.

Marcia Falk

The Typefaces

Basically three different kinds of voices speak these poems: singular male, singular female, and a group of speakers. These voices are usually distinguishable in the original because various parts of speech in Hebrew, including the pronoun "you," have gender and number. So, for example, when a speaker says "I love you" in Hebrew, we know whether a man or a woman is being addressed and, by assuming a heterosexual relationship in these love poems (an assumption validated by the content of the text), we can deduce the gender of the speaker as well. Without such grammatical clues, it would be difficult to know who speaks the various passages in the Song of Songs, particularly because the voices are not stereotypically "male" or "female." Because English does not convey gender in the ways Hebrew does (for example, in English "you" can be either masculine or feminine), the English poems are printed here in three different typefaces. Throughout the book, passages spoken by a female voice are in *italic* (as in poem 1); passages spoken by a male voice are set in roman (as in poem 4); and passages spoken by a a group of voices or by unidentifiable speakers are printed in sans serif (as in poem 11).

Because many of the poems are dialogues and some have multiple speakers, different typefaces appear within individual poems. Within any given poem, each typeface represents a consistent speaker. For example, the female speaker of the first stanza of poem 7 is the same as the speaker of that poem's third stanza. However, the typefaces are not meant to indicate consistent personae among the poems. For example, while *italic* always signifies that a woman is speaking, it is not intended to suggest that the same woman speaks from poem to poem; that is, the woman who speaks in poem 1 is not necessarily the same woman who speaks in poem 2.

The variety of contexts, moods, and arguments among the individual poems in the Song of Songs suggests, I believe, a similarly wide range of speakers. I leave it to the reader to infer what variety of voices comes to life in these lyrics.

O for your kiss! For your love
More enticing than wine,
For your scent and sweet name—
For all this they love you.

Take me away to your room,
Like a king to his rooms—
We'll rejoice there with wine.
No wonder they love you!

Yes, I am black! and radiant—
O city women watching me—
As black as Kedar's goathair tents
Or Solomon's fine tapestries.

Will you disrobe me with your stares?
The eyes of many morning suns
Have pierced my skin, and now I shine
Black as the light before the dawn.

And I have faced the angry glare
Of others, even my mother's sons
Who sent me out to watch their vines
While I neglected all my own.

Tell me, my love, where you feed your sheep
And where you rest in the afternoon,
For why should I go searching blindly
Among the flocks of your friends?

If you don't know, O lovely woman,
Follow the tracks that the sheep have made
And feed your own little goats and lambs
In the fields where the shepherds lie.

Like a mare among stallions,
You lure, I am held

    your cheeks framed with braids
    your neck traced with shells

I'll adorn you with gold
And with silver bells

Until the king returns
*   I lie in fragrance,*
Sweet anticipation
*   Of his entrance.*

Between my breasts he'll lie—
*   Sachet of spices,*
Spray of blossoms plucked
*   From the oasis.*

How fine
you are, my love,
your eyes
like doves'.

*How fine
are you, my lover,
what joy
we have together.*

*How green
our bed of leaves,
our rafters of cedars,
our juniper eaves.*

In sandy earth or deep
In valley soil
I grow, a wildflower thriving
On your love.

Narcissus in the brambles,
Brightest flower—
I choose you from all others
For my love.

Sweet fruit tree growing wild
Within the thickets—
I blossom in your shade
And taste your love.

He brings me to the winehall,
Gazing at me with love.

Feed me raisincakes and quinces!
For I am sick with love.

O for his arms around me,
Beneath me and above.

O women of the city,
Swear by the wild field doe

Not to wake or rouse us
Till we fulfill our love.

The sound of my lover
coming from the hills
quickly, like a deer
upon the mountains

Now at my windows,
walking by the walls,
here at the lattices
he calls—

Come with me,
my love,
come away

For the long wet months are past,
the rains have fed the earth
and left it bright with blossoms

Birds wing in the low sky,
dove and songbird singing
in the open air above

Earth nourishing tree and vine,
green fig and tender grape,
green and tender fragrance

Come with me,
my love,
come away

My dove
    in the clefts
       of the rocks
    the secret
       of steep ravines

Come let me look at you
Come let me hear you

    Your voice clear as water
    Your beautiful body

Catch the foxes!
   the little foxes
   among the vines
Catch the foxes!
   the quick little foxes
   raiding the new grapes
   on our vines

My lover turns to me,
I turn to him,
Who leads his flock to feed
Among the flowers.

Until the day is over
And the shadows flee,
Turn round, my lover,
Go quickly, and be
Like deer or gazelles
In the clefts of the hills.

At night in bed, I want him—
The one I love is not here.

I'll rise and search the city,
Through the streets and squares

Until the city watchmen
Find me wandering there

And I ask them—have you seen him?
The one I love is not here.

When they have gone, I find him
And I won't let him go

Until he's in my mother's home,
The room where I was born.

O women of the city,
Swear by the wild field doe

Not to wake or rouse us
Till we fulfill our love.

Who is this approaching, up from the desert
In columns of smoke, fragrant with incense,
Rare spices and herbs of the wandering merchants?

Behold, it appears—the king's own procession
Attended by sixty of Israel's warriors,
Swords at their thighs to meet the night's dangers.

A carriage of cedar with pillars of silver,
Gold floor, purple cushions, all made to his orders
And fashioned with love by Jerusalem's daughters.

Go out and see, O Jerusalem's daughters!
Crowned by his mother, the king in his carriage
This day of rejoicing, this day of his marriage.

How fine
you are, my love,
your eyes like doves'
behind your veil

Your hair—
as black as goats
winding down the slopes

Your teeth—
a flock of sheep
rising from the stream
in twos, each with its twin

Your lips—
like woven threads
of crimson silk

A gleam of pomegranate—
your forehead
through your veil

Your neck—
a tower
adorned with shields

Your breasts—
twin fawns
in fields of flowers

Until
the day is over,
shadows gone,

I'll go
up to the hills
of fragrant bloom

How fine
you are, my love,
my perfect one

With me, my bride of the mountains,
Come away with me, come away!

Come down from the peaks of the mountains,
From the perilous Lebanon caves,

From the lairs where lions crouch hidden,
Where leopards watch nightly for prey,

Look down, look down and come away!

With one flash of your eyes, you excite me,
One jewel on your neck stirs my heart,
    O my sister, my bride.

Your love, more than wine, is enticing,
Your fragrance is finer than spices,
    My sister, my bride.

Your lips, sweet with nectar, invite me
To honey and milk on your tongue,
    O my sister, my bride.

And even your clothing is fragrant
As wind from the Lebanon mountains,
    My sister, my bride.

Enclosed and hidden, you are a garden,
A still pool, a fountain.

Stretching your limbs, you open—
A field of pomegranates blooms,

Treasured fruit among the blossoms,
Henna, sweet cane, bark, and saffron,

Fragrant woods and succulents,
The finest spices and perfumes.

Living water, you are a fountain,
A well, a river flowing from the mountains.

Come, north winds and south winds!
Breathe upon my garden,

Bear its fragrance to my lover,
Let him come and share its treasures.

My bride, my sister, I have come
To gather spices in my garden,

To taste wild honey with my wine,
Milk and honey with my wine.

Feast, drink—and drink deeply—lovers!

I sleep, but my heart stirs,
restless,
          and dreams . . .

My lover's voice here, at the door—

Open, my love, my sister,
my dove, my perfect one,
for my hair is soaked with the night.

Should I get up, get dressed, and dirty my feet?

My love thrusts his hand at the latch
and my heart leaps for him.
I rise to open for my love,
my hands dripping perfume on the lock.
I open, but he has gone.

I run out after him, calling, but he is gone.

The men who roam the streets,
guarding the walls,
beat me and tear away my robe.

O women of the city,
Swear to me!
If you find my lover
You will say
That I am sick with love.

Who is your love
And why do you bind us by oath?

My love is radiant
As gold or crimson,
Hair in waves of black
Like wings of ravens.

Eyes like doves, afloat
Upon the water,

Bathed in milk, at rest
On brimming pools.

Cheeks like beds of spices,
Banks of flowers,
Lips like lilies, sweet
And wet with dew.

Studded with jewels, his arms
Are round and golden,
His belly smooth as ivory,
Bright with gems.

Set in gold, his legs,
Two marble columns—
He stands as proud as cedars
In the mountains.

Man of pleasure—sweet
To taste his love!
Friend and lover chosen
For my love.

Beautiful woman,
Where has your lover gone to?
Where has he gone?
We'll help you look for him.

My love has gone to walk
Among his gardens—
To feed his sheep and there
To gather flowers.

I turn to meet my love,
He'll turn to me,
Who leads his flock to feed
Among the flowers.

Striking as Tirza
    you are, my love,
Bright as Jerusalem,
    frightening as visions!
Lower your eyes
    for they make me tremble

Your hair—as black as goats
    winding down the slopes
Your teeth—a flock of sheep
    rising from the stream
    in twos, each with its twin
A gleam of pomegranate—
    your forehead through your veil

Sixty queens, eighty brides,
    endless numbers of women—
One is my dove, my perfect one,
    pure as an only child—
Women see her
    and sing of her joy,
Queens and brides
    chant her praise

Who is she? staring
    down like the dawn's eye,
Bright as the white moon,
    pure as the hot sun,
Frightening as visions!

Walking through the walnut orchard,
Looking for the signs of spring:
The pomegranates—have they flowered?
The grapevines—are they blossoming?

Dance for us, princess, dance,
as we watch and chant!

*What will you see as I move
in the dance of love?*

Your graceful, sandalled feet,
Your thighs—two spinning jewels,
Your hips—a bowl of nectar
brimming full

Your belly—golden wheat
Adorned with daffodils,
Your breasts—two fawns, the twins
of a gazelle

Your neck—an ivory tower,
Your eyes—two silent pools,
Your face—a tower that overlooks
the hills

Your head—majestic mountain
Crowned with purple hair,
Captivating kings
within its locks

Of all pleasure, how sweet
Is the taste of love!

There you stand like a palm,
Your breasts clusters of dates.

Shall I climb that palm
And take hold of the boughs?

Your breasts will be tender
As clusters of grapes,

Your breath will be sweet
As the fragrance of quince,

And your mouth will awaken
All sleeping desire

Like wine that entices
The lips of new lovers.

Oh, if you were my brother
Nursed at my mother's breast,

I'd kiss you in the streets
And never suffer scorn.

I'd bring you to my mother's home
(My mother teaches me)

And give you wine and nectar
From my pomegranates.

O for his arms around me,
Beneath me and above!

O women of the city,
Swear by the wild field doe

Not to wake or rouse us
Till we fulfill our love.

Who is this approaching,
    up from the wilderness,
        arm on her lover's arm?

Under the quince tree
  you woke
  to my touch
there
  where she conceived
  where she who carried
  and bore you
conceived

Stamp me in your heart,
Upon your limbs,
Sear my emblem deep
Into your skin.

For love is strong as death,
Harsh as the grave.
Its tongues are flames, a fierce
And holy blaze.

Endless seas and floods,
Torrents and rivers
Never put out love's
Infinite fires.

Those who think that wealth
Can buy them love
Only play the fool
And meet with scorn.

We have a young sister
Whose breasts are but flowers.
What shall we do
When the time comes for suitors?

If she's a wall
We'll build turrets of silver,
But if she's a door
We will plank her with cedar.

I am a wall
And my breasts are towers!
So I have found peace
Here with my lover.

The king has a vineyard
Whose fruit is worth silver.
I have a vineyard—
Its fruit is my own.

Have your wealth, Solomon!
Keep all your vineyards,
Whose yield you must share
With your watchmen and guards.

Woman
of the gardens,
of the voice
friends listen for,
will you let me hear you?

Go—
go now, my love,
be quick
as a gazelle
on the fragrant hills!

About This Translation

One of the most celebrated collections of ancient love poetry, the Song of Songs (also known in English as the Song of Solomon) is the only book of love poems in the Bible, and as such it has been the subject of much speculation and controversy. For centuries, both Jewish and Christian traditions viewed the Song as spiritual allegory, thus justifying its place in the Biblical canon; but this mode of interpretation, moving and imaginative as it may be, is a religious commentary that does not explain the text's primary level of meaning. Another centuries-old interpretation presents the Song as a drama with fixed characters, such as King Solomon and a country bride or King Solomon and two peasant lovers. But it is difficult to find evidence of dramatic structure in the Song: acts, scenarios, and characters are not indicated and there is hardly a trace of coherent plot. Rather, the Song has a wide variety of contexts which shift frequently in no apparent dramatic sequence and within which many different kinds of voices speak. There is no reason to assume only a few fixed speakers in the Song and even less justification for seeing Solomon as a central character. Although Solomon's name is mentioned in the Hebrew title, this title was bestowed not by the Song's original author or authors but by later compilers, who were also responsible for giving the text its semblance of structural unity. In its earliest stages, the Song was probably not a unified work at all but several short lyric poems, each with its own integrity and beauty.

About its authorship and origins very little is known. Tradition ascribes the work to King Solomon but this view is discounted by modern scholars, who generally agree that the Song's authorship cannot be specified. In the past two centuries, scholars have hypothesized about the original context and function of the Song, proposing, for example, that it was a cycle of wedding songs similar to ones found in Syria or that it was the liturgy of an ancient fertility cult. These theories, however, are not only unprovable but unconvincing because they attempt to force the varied material in the text into single, confining molds. It is finally simpler and more illuminating to view the Song as a variegated collection of several different types of poems which do not necessarily derive from the same source or share a single original function. The stylistic similarities and repetitions among the poems are best explained as literary conventions of ancient Hebrew verse, particularly if one accepts the view that the Song was, in its earliest stages, popular oral literature. I believe it likely that the Song was orally composed and transmitted over an extended period of time before being transcribed, compiled, and finally canonized.

The stylistic and thematic features that characterize the collection as a whole give us at least a partial picture of the culture out of which this poetry emerged. For example, the poems express a strikingly nonsexist attitude toward heterosexual love, an attitude that excludes many of our modern Western stereotypes of "masculinity" and "femininity." Both male and female speakers remark upon their lovers' dovelike eyes, and in poem 19 it is a man who has cheeks like spices and lips like lilies. Women initiate lovemaking as often as men; both male and female voices are at times urgent and aggressive, at other times tender and vulnerable. This reciprocity between men and women is surely one of the Song's most inviting aspects and part of its lasting power.

Although the Song is perhaps most appreciated for its appeal to the senses, it is all the more remarkable for its intellectual and emotional complexity. Much of its truth is woven from paradox: in poem 2, blackness is radiant as the very light of the sun; in poem 20, beauty is frightening. Conflicting emotions appear throughout the Song; not all the poems are simply about romantic love nor are all the poetic contexts idyllic. Anxiety, fear, and even hostility are expressed, particularly in those poems which are set in urban contexts. The city seems to be an environment that threatens the love relationship, and implied in this is a contrast between public and private domains. Also suggested is an underlying theme of secret love: in several poems, the female speaker chases her lover away—not because she is rejecting him but because she prefers to postpone their rendezvous until dark, when they can be safely away from the public eye. Sometimes even the world of nature (so beguiling a backdrop in many of the poems) provides an ominous landscape that keeps the lovers apart. Separation of the lovers is a recurrent theme among the poems in the Song, and lovemaking is more often invited, anticipated, and wished for, than actually consummated. Even the last poem in the collection ends on a note of anticipation rather than fulfillment—anticipation of the moment when the lover will return, at night.

Read on the "simplest" level—without delving into allegorical interpretation, without elaborate hypotheses of dramatic structure or contextual unity—the Song reveals itself to be more than a "simple" text. The simple level, in other words, need not be superficial; the Song is classic evidence that popular love poetry need not be slight. While the Song can be enjoyed solely for its surface of sensuous imagery and inventive metaphors, it offers even more to the reader who gives it a second glance, a glance that will (to borrow a metaphor from poem 2) pierce the skin.

But why this new translation of the Song, a book that has been translated, interpreted, arranged, and—to use Franz Rosenzweig's image—"convulsed" many times? By far the most acclaimed English version has been that in the King James Bible which, although it treats the Song no differently from Biblical prose, achieves a level of eloquence and grace that earns it a unique place among English classics. Still, from the perspective of scholarship, the King James Version is long outdated. Our understanding of the Hebrew text has changed considerably since the time of the King James, and one of the offshoots of modern research has been a series of new Bible translations. Unfortunately, the modern translations of the Song lack poetic texture and density, so much so that, for this reason if no other, they cannot be considered faithful renditions of the original. Hence the need to go one step further, to combine scholarship with conscious poetic craft and sensibility. This translation is an attempt to fill that need.

I was aware, from the very outset, of the great impact that the King James Version has had on the ears of English readers. Rather than trying to echo its rhythms or diction, I set out to create an entirely fresh version, one that would open up the locked gardens of the Hebrew and give them new life in the American terrain. My aim was to probe the roots of the original and uncover the resonances lost in other translations, but *not* to "Hebraize" English or mimic the aesthetic techniques of Hebrew verse. Rather than writing "translationese," I tried to write the best poetry I could.

All translations are, by necessity, interpretations. My division of the text into thirty-one poems is, in itself, the result of literary interpretation and structural analysis. Although most scholars today view the Song as a collection of several poems, the particular decisions concerning where one poem ends and the next begins are not at all obvious, and no two analyses are exactly alike. The text, as we have it in the oldest complete manuscript of the Hebrew Bible (Leningrad MS., 11th century), is divided into sections which may have been considered poetic units, but these divisions can hardly be regarded as definitive delineations of the original, orally transmitted poems. Therefore, every reconstruction of the text is, at best, a postulation of the boundaries of the original poems. I divided the Hebrew text into poems as I perceived them, basing my decisions on such considerations as changes in settings, speakers, attitudes, moods, and arguments. I then rendered the Hebrew poems individually, trying to give each an integral form in English. The Hebrew text I translated from was the one printed in *Biblia Hebraica* (eds. Kittel and Kahle, 7th ed., 1951), without emendations or alteration of the sequence. I translated the entire text of the Song with the exception of chapter 6, verse 12, a line which has plagued commentators for centuries and for which I could arrive at no satisfactory interpretation. Following this note is a chart indicating the Biblical chapters and verses to which each poem corresponds.

The translations of the individual poems also reflect my interpretations which, though necessarily subjective, are grounded in linguistic research, literary analysis, and, at times, investigation of other ancient Near Eastern sources.*

* The reader interested in my sources and the arguments for my interpretations can find them in my doctoral dissertation, "The Song of Songs: A Verse Translation with Exposition" (Stanford University, 1976), available from University Microfilms, Ann Arbor, Michigan.

While none of the translations is literal—neither word for word nor line by line—all are attempts to draw closer to the meanings, intentions, and spirit of their Hebrew counterparts. My aim was fidelity—not to isolated images but to the meanings of those images in their contexts and to the effects they might have had upon their earliest audience. Thus, at times, my renditions will seem to depart quite radically from other, more literal versions.

For example, in chapter 1, verse 9 of the Hebrew (the opening lines of poem 4 here), the woman is compared to a mare among Pharaoh's chariots. A puzzling image: mares did not draw chariots. But the Egyptians' enemies set mares loose in war to drive the Pharaoh's stallions wild, and this is the crux of the metaphor. The woman is not simply as beautiful as a regal horse; she is as alluring as "a mare among stallions." Thus the image unfolds on two levels and, once again, paradox is implied: the woman is a graceful creature, a quiet profile, yet also a dangerous, captivating power. Seen this way, the image also ties in nicely with the rest of the poem, which is built on the subtle paradox of the love relationship: although the beloved is beautiful just as she is, the speaker, wanting to share love, offers to adorn her with his own gifts.

The poems in this book are a gift back to their source, and an attempt to share in the tradition.

Marcia Falk
New York, 1977

Chart of Biblical Chapter and Verse References

Poem Number	Biblical Chapter and Verse
1	1:2–4*
2	1:5–6
3	1:7–8
4	1:9–11
5	1:12–14
6	1:15–17
7	2:1–3
8	2:4–7
9	2:8–13
10	2:14
11	2:15
12	2:16–17
13	3:1–5
14	3:6–11
15	4:1–7
16	4:8
17	4:9–11
18	4:12–5:1
19	5:2–6:3
20	6:4–10
21	6:11**
22	7:1–6
23	7:7–10
24	7:11–14
25	8:1–4
26	8:5a
27	8:5b
28	8:6–7
29	8:8–10
30	8:11–12
31	8:13–14

* 1:1 of the Hebrew is the title of the work, usually referred to in English as "the Song of Songs" or "the Song of Solomon" (literally, "the Song of Songs which is Solomon's"), and commonly abbreviated "the Song."

** 6:12 of the Hebrew has not been translated because its meaning is not decipherable.

Marcia Falk was born in New York City in 1946. A poet, translator, and painter, she studied art at the Art Students League of New York, philosophy at Brandeis University, and English and Comparative Literature at Stanford University, where she received a Ph.D. She was a Fulbright scholar to Israel in 1973–74 and was recently awarded a postdoctoral fellowship to the Hebrew University in Jerusalem. She has published a book of translations of the Yiddish poet Malka Heifetz Tussman, *Am I Also You?*, and her own poems and translations in numerous magazines and anthologies. Currently an Assistant Professor of English and Hebrew at the State University of New York at Binghamton, Marcia Falk is now at work on a collection of her own poems.

This book was set in ten point Palatino roman,
ten point Palatino italics, and nine point Helvetica roman.
It was printed by offset on Perkins and Squire offset wove
manufactured by the P. H. Glatfelter Company.
The cover materials are Kennett Cloth manufactured
by Joanna Western, and multicolor paper
supplied by Lindenmeyr Paper Company.
Original drawings by Barry Moser.
Printed and bound by The Book Press.
Book design by Kay Lee.